# ENDANGERED!

# LEOPARDS

## Amanda Harman

Series Consultant: James G. Doherty
General Curator, The Bronx Zoo, New York

BENCHMARK BOOKS

MARSHALL CAVENDISH
NEW YORK

Benchmark Books
Marshall Cavendish Corporation
99 White Plains Road
Tarrytown, New York 10591-9001

©Marshall Cavendish Corporation, 1996

Library of Congress Cataloging-in-Publication Data

Harman, Amanda, 1968-
    Leopards / Amanda Harman.
        p.    cm. — (Endangered!)
    Includes bibliographical references (p.      ) and index.
    Summary: Discusses how these magnificent cats live and what is
being done to keep them from disappearing in the wild.
    ISBN 0-7614-0223-3  ( lib.  bdg.)
    1.  Leopard—Juvenile literature.  2.  Endangered species—Juvenile
literature.  [1.  Leopard.  2.  Endangered species.]  I.  Title.
II.  Series.
QL737.C23H357  1996
599.74'428—dc20                                    95-47542
                                                      CIP
                                                       AC

Printed in Hong Kong

**PICTURE CREDITS**
*The publishers would like to thank the Frank Lane Picture Agency for
supplying all the photographs used in this book.*

Series created by Brown Packaging

Front cover: Leopard.
Title page: Snow leopard and cub.
Back cover: Snow leopard.

# Contents

# Introduction

Leopards are large and powerful. They are beautiful animals that look like huge, spotted pet cats as they snooze the day away in a favorite spot. But these close cousins of lions and tigers are also ferocious hunters. They are **carnivores** and must hunt and eat other animals to live.

Although most people think of only one kind of large cat when they hear the name "leopard," there are really three different **species**. Besides the "true" leopard, there are the snow leopard and clouded leopard. The snow leopard is

*A leopard watches from a leafy perch. During the heat of the day, leopards often stretch out in a shady place and rest.*

closely related to the true leopard. The clouded leopard is a little different than the other two. But it is fairly large and has a spotted coat, so people call it a leopard.

All three cats are now in danger of becoming **extinct**. Other types of cats have disappeared in the past for natural reasons. But today leopards are threatened not by natural changes but by human beings. Many, many leopards have been killed so that people could wear their skins as coats. In this book we will look at the three kinds of leopards to learn how they live and what is being done to stop these magnificent creatures from vanishing forever.

*The snow leopard lives where the weather is very harsh in the winter. Its beautiful coat grows thicker to protect it from the snow and bitter cold.*

# Leopard

The leopard is a graceful, athletic cat. Its coat is usually yellow to gray-brown in color and covered completely with single dark spots and clusters of spots, known as rosettes.

Leopards have one of the largest **ranges** of any cat. They are scattered across most of Africa and can be found in southern and eastern Asia. Leopards from different areas often differ slightly from one another, so scientists usually look at them as a number of separate **subspecies**. Experts do not see eye to eye on just how many subspecies there are, though.

*Leopards are about 8 feet 9 inches (2.7 m) long, including the tail. Males are usually larger than females and weigh up to 155 pounds (70 kg).*

Among the subspecies is the Amur leopard, which is found in Korea, northeastern China, and a small area of southeastern Russia. It has long, pale fur with large spots. Another is the Zanzibar leopard. This subspecies is probably now extinct but had very small spots and used to live on the island of Zanzibar, just off the east coast of Africa. Other subspecies include the North African, Anatolian, Barbary, Sinai, and South Arabian leopards.

Although leopards are usually yellowish in color, some are completely black. Often called black panthers, these black-coated leopards are usually found in Asia, especially in forest and mountain **habitats**.

*Areas where the leopard can be found*

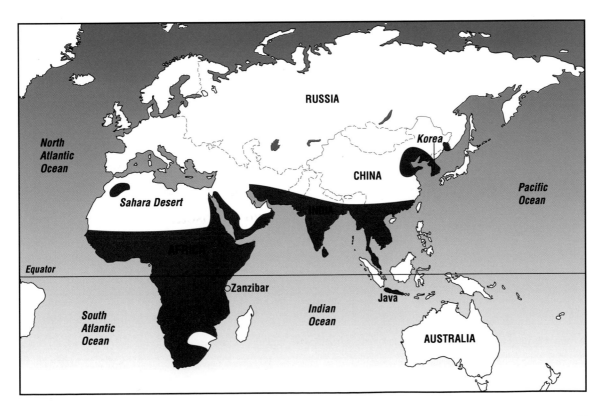

7

Leopards are **adapted** to living in a wide variety of habitats within their range. They may be found in **tropical** forests and swamps or in dry grasslands and deserts. Leopards that live in forests are particularly good climbers, using their strong legs to leap high up a tree trunk and their sharp claws to cling to the bark as they go. Climbing among the branches, they are hard to see. Their spotted coats hide them well, blending in with the speckled pattern the sunlight makes as it shines through the leaves.

*Black panthers are not a separate species of cat. They are not even a distinct subspecies. They are simply leopards that are born with black fur.*

Leopards are skillful hunters. Some hunt during the day, usually at dawn or dusk, when the air is cooler and they can hide among the shadows. Most, though, are active in the dead of night. Leopards use a number of methods to catch their **prey**. Sometimes they may climb trees and snatch guinea fowl from their perches. Or they may clamber through the branches, trying to frighten young baboons into losing their footing and falling to their death.

The leopard's main hunting method, though, is to sneak up silently on its prey. With its body crouched low to the ground and its eyes fixed on the animal, the leopard creeps closer and closer until it is near enough to pounce. Leopards have very long, sensitive whiskers to help them

*A leopard pounces on a young impala, a kind of antelope. Leopards eat many different foods. Besides antelope, their diet includes deer, wild pigs, baboons, and birds.*

feel their way through the undergrowth in the dark. And they can see up to six times better than people.

Even so, getting close to its prey can be very difficult for a leopard. Animals can usually tell when a leopard is around and are alert and wary. It may take many attempts before the leopard can get near enough. But as soon as it does, it rushes forward and grabs the victim with its front paws. It then closes its jaws around the animal's throat so that it cannot breathe or breaks its neck as the two of them roll over on the ground. Once the leopard has caught and killed its prey, it usually drags the carcass up into the branches of a tree. This shows just how strong the leopard is – sometimes the prey is as big as the leopard itself!

*A leopard clamps its teeth around the throat of a Thomson's gazelle. This stops the prey from breathing, and it soon dies.*

These amazing hunters usually live alone. Each occupies a **territory**, which may cover more than 11 square miles (30 sq km). A leopard spends much of its time patrolling the boundaries of its territory, spraying logs and trees with urine. A leopard's urine contains a special scent that tells other leopards the area is occupied. Usually this is enough to keep a stranger out. Sometimes, though, a leopard does wander into another's territory. The owner will not stand for this, and a serious fight may break out.

*This leopard has hauled its zebra kill up a tree to keep it safe from other animals. Hyenas and wild dogs hunt in groups and could easily rob a solitary leopard of its food. But neither of them are able to climb trees.*

11

# Leopard

Although leopards are solitary animals, males and females get together briefly to **mate**. Leopards can breed by the time they are four years old. When she is ready to mate, the female calls with a rasping growl, and a nearby male visits her. After they have mated, the male leaves the female and returns to his own territory.

Nearly four months after mating, the female gives birth to a litter of up to six cubs. They are already covered with fur, which looks almost gray because the dark spots are so close together. The cubs weigh less than 1.5 pounds (680 g) at birth and are blind and helpless for about nine days. Cats are **mammals**, and so the mother feeds her newborns on milk. She keeps them hidden in a **den**, where they are safe from hunters such as bears, lions, tigers, and wolves.

*When her cubs are still small, the female leopard carries them gently in her mouth. Here a mother brings one of her cubs from the den.*

*A leopard cub clambers up a tree in the Masai Mara National Park, Kenya. Leopards learn to climb at an early age.*

Once they are about eight weeks old, the cubs leave the den. They follow their mother on hunting trips and start to share in her kills. Already they are starting to pick up all the hunting skills they will need. First they stalk mice and rats, then move on to larger prey as they grow. By the time they reach two years old, the cubs are big enough and skilled enough to leave their mother and find their own territories. In the wild, leopards probably live for about 15 years – in a zoo they may reach the age of 23.

Human actions have put many leopard subspecies in danger. In some cases it is hard to blame people for killing them. When farmers move into areas where leopards live, the cats will attack and eat their livestock. Also, there have been cases of leopards attacking people. For these reasons, farmers and villagers will often shoot a leopard on sight if it is seen anywhere near their homes and farms.

However, the greatest threat to the leopard is from hunting. People have shot many leopards in order to show off their skins as trophies. And many more have been killed so that their skins could be sold to the fur trade. During the early 1960s, as many as 50,000 leopards were killed in East Africa alone.

*The skin of a leopard killed for its fur. People have long loved to wear the beautiful, spotted fur of the leopard. But it takes the skins of up to seven leopards to make just one fur coat!*

14

It is now illegal to shoot leopards for their fur, but **poachers** still kill them in the thousands. In Africa south of the Sahara, leopards are more plentiful than in other parts of their range, although they have vanished from some places. Elsewhere, the leopard is in very serious danger. Besides the probably extinct Zanzibar leopard, the rarest subspecies is the Amur leopard. Many of the surviving Russian Amur leopards live in a protected area called the Kedrovaya Pad Nature Reserve. Sadly, though, poaching goes on even there. **Conservationists** have started the Far East Leopard Fund to raise money to pay guards and to open a second **reserve**. They also want to study Amur leopards to learn how to care for them better in the future.

*The Amur leopard is in serious danger of becoming extinct. Scientists believe there may be only 30 of them left in Russia and a few more in China and Korea.*

Areas where the
snow leopard can
be found

*Also known as
the ounce, the
snow leopard
is a powerful
hunter, but it
has never
been known
to attack
a person.*

# Snow Leopard

The snow leopard is similar in size and shape to the true leopard. It measures up to 4 feet 4 inches (1.3 m) from head to rump and has a long, furry tail that it can wrap around itself when it goes to sleep in cold weather. Snow leopards are usually under 110 pounds (50 kg), although they may weigh as much as 155 pounds (70 kg).

The snow leopard is found in some mountainous parts of Asia, where it is hot in summer and very cold in winter. However, the snow leopard is adapted to its harsh habitat. Besides having a thick fur coat, it has a large nose with wide nostrils. When the cat breathes in, the cold air circulates in its nostrils and warms up before it passes into the animal's lungs. The snow leopard's paws are very broad and act just like snow shoes to keep it from sinking into the deep snow. And the soles of its paws have thick pads and tufts of hair to protect them from both the freezing snow in winter and the hot, sun-baked rocks in summer.

Like true leopards, snow leopards are solitary animals. For the most part, the only snow leopards seen together are

*During the summer, the snow leopard lives high on rocky mountain slopes. But in winter, the snow leopard moves down the mountains, sometimes into thick forests.*

adult males and females during the mating season, or females with their cubs. And they have very large home areas of more than 36 square miles (95 sq km). Snow leopards are very alert and tend to stay away from people. All this explains why they are so difficult to study. Often scientists have to follow tracks in the snow for many miles before they can sight one of these shy, secretive creatures.

Once they reach the age of two, snow leopards are able to breed. The breeding season is in late winter and early spring, between the months of January and May. At this time, adult males and females get together for a short time to mate and then go their separate ways once again. About 14 weeks after mating, the female gives birth to a litter of

*Snow leopards can be hard to find. One way to tell if one has passed by is to look for tail marks. The snow leopard's tail often drags behind it, leaving a long groove in the snow.*

cubs. They are totally helpless at first – they can crawl around but are blind and only about 1 pound (450 g) in weight. To begin with, the cubs' fur is much darker than their mother's, and their spots are completely black.

After about a week, the young snow leopards open their eyes for the first time. They are fully active at two months and can eat solid food as well as drinking their mother's milk. By midsummer, they are ready to leave the safety of the den. The cubs probably stay with their mother until they are about two years old, and then leave to start their own solitary lives.

*A snow leopard cub and its mother nuzzle each other. There are usually two or three cubs in a snow leopard litter, although there may be as many as five.*

Snow leopards are active mainly in the early morning and late afternoon. Most of these hours are spent finding and hunting prey. Like the true leopard, the snow leopard often hunts its victims by stalking them silently. It is ideally suited to this way of hunting. The cat's silvery or creamy gray fur helps it blend in among the rocks and snow when it needs to. And because its eyes are positioned high on its head, the snow leopard is able to hide behind large rocks and peer over at its prey. Once it is about 30 feet (9 m) away, the crouching cat pushes off with its strong hind legs and leaps on to the unsuspecting animal.

Sometimes, though, the snow leopard ambushes its prey instead of stalking it. It chooses a high rocky crag and then

*A snow leopard relaxes on a rock. Snow leopards' coats vary from very pale silvery gray to creamy, smoky yellow and are dotted with small, dark spots and rosettes.*

lies down and waits. When an animal passes by, the cat drops on it from above.

One problem for the snow leopard is that people track down many of its prey, leaving it with too little food. For example, the gray marmot is shot and its skin sold for about $3. Faced with a shortage of natural prey, snow leopards will attack farm animals and pets belonging to people who live in the mountains. This has made them enemies of the local people, who shoot these beautiful, spotted cats on sight.

*The snow leopard's favorite foods are wild goats, gazelles, deer, and wild pigs. But it also eats birds and small mammals such as hares.*

## Snow Leopard

Some people also kill snow leopards for their fur. A snow leopard's luxurious, thick coat is still worth a lot, even though buying and selling its fur is now banned. Just one skin can be worth more than $3000.

The result is that the snow leopard is in very serious danger. About 400 live in zoos around the world, but no one knows exactly how many survive in the wild. Their shyness and the wildness of the habitat in which they live make snow leopards difficult to count. Conservationists think there could be as many as 10,000 wild snow leopards left, but the number might be as low as 1000.

*People keep turning more of the snow leopard's habitat into farmland, making the cat's natural prey even more scarce.*

*A litter of snow leopard cubs with their keeper at a zoo in England.*

Conservationists have suggested a number of measures to save the snow leopard. These include setting up protected areas for snow leopards and starting a campaign to tell the public about the problems faced by this beautiful cat. In 1990, India started Project Snow Leopard, which raises money to set up parks and reserves where snow leopards can be protected from poachers.

Areas where the
clouded leopard can
be found

# Clouded Leopard

The clouded leopard has slightly different markings from other leopards. Instead of having small spots and rosettes, its coat is marked with large, gray, cloud-shaped blotches surrounded by black rings. Black stripes cover its head and run down its neck and the middle of its back. All-black clouded leopards have been sighted, but these are rare.

Clouded leopards are found in southern Asia and on the islands of Sumatra and Borneo. They live in thick tropical **rainforests**, in lowlands as well as in higher mountainous

*The clouded leopard is smaller than other leopards. It is about 6 feet 6 inches (2 m) long from head to tail.*

country. Clouded leopards are excellent climbers. Like true leopards, they use their strong, sharp claws to haul themselves up trees and their long tail to help them balance on branches.

During the hottest part of the day, the clouded leopard rests high in the trees, draped along the branches or nestled in the fork of a tree. Then, at dusk, when many of its prey are settling down for the night, the clouded leopard goes hunting. It spends even more of its time in the trees than the true leopard does, hunting small creatures, such as birds, insects, mice, snakes, and monkeys.

*Clouded leopards are well adapted to their forest habitat. Their markings help them to blend in with their surroundings as they search for food among the thick vegetation.*

Sometimes the clouded leopard ambushes its prey by dropping out of the trees. Clouded leopards have been seen to hang from a branch by one back paw as they take aim at the victim passing by below. They also hunt on the ground, searching out small deer and wild pigs. In Borneo and Sumatra, they have been known to kill young orangutans. To kill its prey, the clouded leopard usually sinks its unusually long **canine teeth** into the animal's neck.

*For its size, the clouded leopard has the biggest canine teeth of any cat. They can be up to 2 inches (5 cm) long.*

*When they feed, clouded leopards use their canine teeth to tear pieces of meat from their victim. Here a clouded leopard bites into a young swamp deer it has killed.*

Numbers of clouded leopards have dropped sharply because of fur hunting. Buying and selling clouded leopard skins is banned, and the cat is protected throughout much of its range, but poaching still goes on. A single clouded leopard skin can bring a hunter up to $2000.

The biggest threat facing clouded leopards is the fact that their habitat is shrinking. In some parts of this leopard's range, people have been cutting down the rainforests to make way for farms and villages. This leaves clouded leopards only small patches of forest in which to live.

Clouded leopards are already found in a number of protected areas, such as national parks and reserves. But for

*Besides being hunted for the fur trade, clouded leopards are also shot and poisoned as pests because they often eat domestic birds, such as chickens.*

the clouded leopard to survive, logging needs to be managed so that whole forests are not destroyed at once. If loggers will not leave enough trees for clouded leopards to live in, more land will need to be set aside as reserves. First, though, scientists have to find out exactly where these shy cats live. Poaching also needs to be controlled.

It has been suggested that people be kept away from known clouded leopard areas so that the cats are not killed. In addition, conservationists would like to see programs to teach people about clouded leopards. They believe that if people understand the cats better they may treat them better in the future.

All three species of leopards are in danger. People are crowding them out of their habitat, killing leopards' prey, and shooting and poisoning leopards as pests. Hunters have also trapped leopards because people could not resist the cats' beautiful fur. If leopards are to survive in the wild, the needs of both people and leopards have to be met. Conservationists are trying to find ways for them to live in peace so that the leopards of the future will survive outside protected areas and zoos.

*A young clouded leopard in its forest home. Unlike the true leopard, the clouded leopard cannot roar. In fact it purrs like a huge pet cat.*

# Useful Addresses

For more information about leopards and how you can help protect them, contact these organizations:

**Conservation International**
1015 18th Street NW
Suite 1000
Washington, D.C. 20036

**Defenders of Wildlife**
1244 19th Street NW
Washington, D.C. 20036

**International Snow Leopard Trust**
4649 Sunnyside Avenue N, Suite 325
Seattle, WA 98103

**U.S. Fish and Wildlife Service**
Endangered Species and Habitat
Conservation
400 Arlington Square
18th and C Streets NW
Washington, D.C. 20240

**The Wildlife Conservation Society**
185th Street and Southern Boulevard
Bronx, New York 10460

**Wildlife Preservation Trust
International**
3400 W Girard Avenue
Philadelphia, PA 19104

**World Wildlife Fund**
1250 24th Street NW
Washington, D.C. 20037

# Further Reading

*Big Cats* Norman Barrett (New York: Franklin Watts, 1988)

*Endangered Mountain Animals* Dave Taylor (New York: Crabtree, 1992)

*Endangered Wildlife of the World* (New York: Marshall Cavendish Corporation, 1993)

*Lions and Tigers and Leopards: The Big Cats* Jennifer C. Urquhart (Washington, D.C.:
     National Geographic Society, 1990)

*Save the Snow Leopard* Jill Bailey (Austin, TX: Raintree Steck-Vaughn, 1992)

*Saving Endangered Mammals* Thane Maynard (New York: Franklin Watts, 1992)

*Wildlife of the World* (New York: Marshall Cavendish Corporation, 1994)

# Glossary

**Adapt**: To change in order to survive in new conditions.

**Canine teeth**: The four large, pointed teeth found at the front corners of a carnivore's mouth. There are two in the upper jaw and two in the lower.

**Carnivore**: A meat-eating animal.

**Conservationist** (Kon-ser-VAY-shun-ist): A person who protects and preserves the Earth's natural resources, such as animals, plants, and soil.

**Den**: A hole or cave that an animal uses as its home.

**Extinct** (Ex-TINKT): No longer living anywhere in the world.

**Habitat**: The place where an animal lives. The snow leopard's habitat is the mountains.

**Mammal**: A kind of animal that is warm-blooded and has a backbone. Most are covered with fur or have hair. Females have glands that produce milk to feed their young.

**Mate**: When a male and female get together to produce young.

**Poacher**: A person who hunts animals even though it is against the law.

**Prey**: An animal that is hunted and eaten by another animal.

**Rainforest**: A forest that has heavy rainfall much of the year.

**Range**: The area in the world in which a particular kind of animal can be found.

**Reserve**: Land that has been set aside where plants and animals can live without being harmed.

**Species**: A kind of animal or plant. For example, the leopard is a species of cat.

**Subspecies**: A group within a species. For example, the Amur leopard is a subspecies of the leopard.

**Territory**: The piece of land in which an animal lives. Some animals, such as leopards, defend their territory against others of their own kind.

**Tropical**: Having to do with or found in the tropics, the region of the Earth near the Equator.

# Index